D1104059

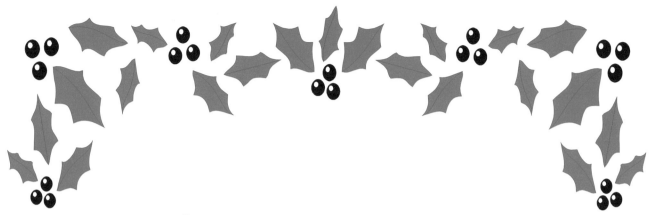

Santa's Secret

by Johanna Daniels

Illustrations by Jay Pittman

This book belongs to:

Mountaintop Press

Mountaintop Press
P.O. Box 550
Cary, N.C. 27512-0550

Santa's Secret
Library of Congress Control Number: 2001118592

Published in the United States by Mountaintop Press

Printed in the United States of America
ISBN 0-9711106-5-4

Santa's workshop was enormous and full of hard working Elves of all ages. The main section was divided into different areas where the toys were made. Parts were put together, pieces were painted, and bicycles were assembled. There were horns tooting, trains whistling, dolls talking, and wheels spinning. Everyone was busy. It was a fun place to be, because everybody was happy.

Captain Clyde was the head Elf. He was in charge of all the workshops. His beard was almost as white as Santa's. He and Santa had worked together for a long time. Captain Clyde's wife, Betsy, helped Mrs. Claus pick which colors to use for the toys.

The door flew open, and the Captain ran into the workshop. He grabbed the rope and rang the bell to call the elves together for a meeting.

"It's not time to meet," curly-haired Anna said. "Is something wrong?"

"I don't know. Let's go find out," Larry, one of the newest elves, answered.

All of the elves stopped what they were doing and gathered around the platform where Captain Clyde waited. Of course, the elves coming from the painting section were the last to arrive, because they had to put lids on the paint cans and clean their brushes. Everyone knew it must have been important for Captain Clyde to interrupt their work.

"Thank you for coming so quickly," Captain Clyde said. "I've just come from Santa's office. He needs our help to solve a problem, and he will be coming to talk with us." Captain Clyde began stroking his beard the way he had watched Santa do for many years.

"Before Santa gets here, I want to make sure all of you new elves know the things you need to understand and understand the things you need to know. Who can tell me what Christmas is?"

Larry got excited because he knew the answer. "It's the day we celebrate Jesus being born," he said.

"That's right," the Captain answered. "But why do we celebrate the birth of Jesus?"

Larry got excited again and answered before anyone else had a chance to speak. "Because of all the wonderful things He taught and did," Larry said.

Anna walked closer to Captain Clyde. "He taught us to be kind to each other, and to forgive each other when we make mistakes," she said.

Beverly, the tiniest elf of all, stopped twiddling her hair. She looked at Larry and Anna. Then she turned to the Captain. "We shouldn't tell lies, we shouldn't steal, and we shouldn't be mean. Jesus taught us to love each other the way we love ourselves," Beverly said.

Captain Clyde raised both arms in the air. "Very good," he cheered. "You are all right. Keep going. What else?"

"He taught us to pray and that we are never alone," said Bobby.

A voice came from the very back, but the Captain could not hear what was said. "What did you say? Who was that?" Captain Clyde asked.

An elf with big, brown eyes stepped forward. "It was me, Steven. Jesus taught us to give. Not just *stuff* but to give what really counts–to give of ourselves. He gave His life for us. He died for us. He is the Savior, because He saved all of us," Steven said.

"What does that mean?" asked the Captain.

Suddenly, there was a huge explosion.

Kerboom! Kerbang! Kerbash! Clink, clink, clink. Clank, clank, clank. Kerplunk! Glops of paint flew across the room as blobs dripped from the ceiling, and plops splattered on the floor.

Captain Clyde raced down the steps and across the floor to the paint section. All the elves followed. The hundreds of finished toys lining rows of shelves were now covered with bright blue paint.

"Oh, dear," Captain Clyde gasped. He could not believe his eyes. There were mishaps from time to time, but in all the years he had been at Santa's workshop, he had never seen anything like this.

Larry, being new, left the welding torch burning. It had rolled under the paint drum. The paint got so hot that it started to boil and finally exploded.

"I feel awful! I am soooo sorry," Larry said. "I never meant for this to happen."

Ralph, the paint shop foreman, was furious. "That's it! You are out of here! I don't want you anywhere near this workshop ever again!" Ralph shouted.

Anna came to Larry's defense. "Ralph, you don't mean that. We all make mistakes sometimes." Anna looked around at the toys. "This one just made a really big mess," she said.

Bradford, the tallest elf in the shop, stepped next to Anna. "Look, I've got some stuff that will clean up most of this mess. It will be okay," he said.

"Why should you clean it up?" Ralph asked. "Larry should…" Ralph stopped and looked at Captain Clyde who had one eyebrow raised. Ralph remembered a mistake he made many years ago that Captain Clyde fixed.

Ralph changed his tone of voice. "That will be fine. Who wants to help Bradford?"

Every elf's hand went up. Ralph was not surprised, because the elves were very good about helping each other. Ralph motioned toward the group on the right.

"Okay, this section go with Bradford," Ralph said. "We'll fill you in on the meeting when you come back."

"Thanks," Bradford replied, and left with his helpers to clean up the paint before it dried.

The door opened and the bells hanging on the knob jingled a happy sound.

"Ho, Ho, Ho," Santa said entering the workshop.

Captain Clyde motioned the group back to the platform. "On to Santa's problem," he said.

Santa walked across the platform, down the steps, pulled up a chair and sat down. Captain Clyde stepped back onto the platform. He thought the elves could hear him better when he stood up there. Everyone gathered around.

Santa began. "For all you new arrivals, let me tell you how this workshop got started. Many years ago, when I was called Nicholas or Nick, I became a Christian. I learned how much Jesus had given to us and for us. So much joy came into my life.

"Well, when Christmas came around that year, I thought long and hard about what it meant. I saw all the people giving and receiving gifts. Then I thought about how Jesus just *gave*…to all of us. There was a poor family down the street, so I decided to give the children presents."

Santa paused, leaned forward, and lowered his voice. "But I didn't want anyone to know they were from me."

He sat back and continued. "I thought if I could make people happy they would pass on the joy and the world would be a better place. The experience brought me so much happiness that I had to do it again…and again," Santa said.

"And again!" Captain Clyde exclaimed.

Smiling, Santa continued. "Well, people eventually found out my secret."

Captain Clyde cleared his throat. "Uh-hum. Actually, he got arrested.
They thought he was stealing from the houses rather than leaving gifts!" he said.

Santa laughed. "That's right." He put his arm around the Captain. "And it was my good friend Clyde here that came to my rescue. The months that followed were hard. Most of my so-called friends thought I was crazy, but Clyde was always there for me."

Clyde blushed. "And Santa was always there for me when people made fun of me being so small. He wrote me a letter and called me his **Ever Loyal Friend**. That's where 'ELF' came from. But all of you already know that.

"I asked Nick, Santa that is, if I could join him. We decided to spread as much joy as we possibly could every Christmas. Santa even asked his wife to make him a suit that was red from the top of his head to the tip of his toes." Clyde stopped and turned to Santa. "Take off your shoes and show them the toes of your socks."

Santa frowned. "Trust me, they're red," he said.

Clyde nudged Santa with his elbow. "Stinky foot problem or is it just too hard bending over to get the old boots off?" he asked.

Santa's mouth dropped. Clyde touched Santa's arm. "Just kidding. Lighten up," he said.

Santa began talking. "The red of my suit represents the blood of Christ. We all were washed clean of our sins and mistakes through the atoning blood of Jesus. Every time I give, I want to remember that He is why I started this tradition."

"What does atoning mean?" one of the elves asked.

"To atone means to make up for something. Jesus made up for all the sins and mistakes we make when He gave His life," Santa said.

Captain Clyde got excited. "Kind of like Bradford cleaning up Larry's mess. Larry was really sorry for what he did and now Bradford is taking care of it. Well, Jesus has taken care of all the messes and mistakes that everybody makes. That is, the ones we are truly sorry for. That's why we're able to go back to our Heavenly Father, and why we celebrate Christmas, Jesus's birthday."

Santa nodded. "That's right. But we have a big problem. A lot of people have forgotten what Christmas is really all about. Instead of the joy of giving, it's all about getting! That is what Christmas has become to millions of children! Even many of the adults have forgotten the true meaning of Christmas. We need ideas to help turn it all around. We need the true meaning and joy of Christmas back!"

Clyde started pacing. "Think, think. We've got to think of something. Some people know that the evergreen tree stands for everlasting life, that the candy canes represent the shepherd's staff, and holly is used to remember Jesus's crown of thorns and drops of blood. But nobody knows that Santa has a secret. He's got a really big secret."

"Please tell us. We want to know," Erma said.

Captain Clyde hesitated.

"Go ahead, Clyde. You can tell them," Santa said.

Clyde smiled a big grin and gave a thumbs-up. He was anxious to let the elves in on this special secret.

"First of all, remember how we came up with ELF, when Santa wrote that I was his Ever Loyal Friend?" The elves nodded yes and listened intently. "Well, Nick, I mean Santa, wanted to make sure no one ever forgot what we were doing and why. SANTA really stands for Savior's Atonement–Necessity To All. We have never forgotten what Christmas is all about. But almost everyone else sure has!" he said.

"What can we do?" Santa asked. "We need ideas. We've got to get the true meaning back in Christmas."

The elves thought and thought, but kept coming up with really bad ideas. They wanted to solve this problem, but it was much harder than it seemed.

"We're never going to come up with anything," Thomas said, with his arms folded and foot tapping.

Melanie patted Thomas's arm. "We can't give up. We'll think of something," she replied

"You're right. We just haven't thought of it yet," blue-eyed Will said smiling.

"I know. Let's shut down the workshop and not give anybody presents. That should get their attention," Elizabeth said scowling, and stomped her foot.

"What?" Captain Clyde gasped.

"I certainly hope it never comes to that! Then we wouldn't be sharing or giving, either," Santa said. "Any other ideas?"

A voice came from the very back. It was cute, little, freckled-face Mark. "Maybe we should tell them about Santa's secret. Everybody's always writing letters to Santa, maybe Santa should write a letter to them," he said.

Santa jumped up. "That's it! Great idea! We'll ask all the kids to help. We've had adult helpers for years–why not the children. Let's do it!"

"Yeah!" Captain Clyde said. "Now the kids can be part of the team."

"Terrific!" Santa said.

Santa and a group of elves worked for days writing *The Letter*. Captain Clyde called a meeting to see what the elves thought of what they had written.

"It's very hard to get so much information into one short letter, but let's see how it sounds. It needs to get out as soon as possible." Captain Clyde began reading *The Letter*,

"Dear boys and girls,

I am writing to you because *I need your help!*

Many people have an emptiness and sadness inside throughout the year because they have forgotten the true magic of Christmas. Somehow the true meaning of Christmas has been lost. Do you know what Christmas is really about?

Christmas is the celebration of the birth of Jesus Christ. *He* should be what we think about first, but people have forgotten. The lights, the decorations, the sparkle, and the excitement are all wonderful! Christmas should be magical. But almost everyone has been distracted from the true meaning of Christmas. What's important is to remember all that Jesus taught during His life and the sacrifices He made for us all. We celebrate His birth to commemorate His life, His example, and His death. That's why the first part of Christmas spells Christ.

Now that you understand the importance of Christmas, I must explain my role. A long time ago, I decided to give gifts in secret on the eve of Jesus' birth. I felt I could sacrifice a little time and money since Jesus sacrificed so much. The Savior's atonement is a necessity to all, so I knew I had to give every year. And that's when it hit me. The Savior's Atonement–Necessity To All: SANTA! From then on, I called myself Santa.

We need to regain the true joy that has been lost. We should be sharing the joy of giving and loving…not just exchanging stuff.

There are many ways to give of yourself–a smile or a hug. You can write a letter or a poem, draw a picture, spend time visiting, lend a helping hand, take time to listen, and many more I am sure you can think of.

We need the special warm feeling of Christmases past. We won't find it in shopping malls or fancy packages. It is in the heart. And it takes much more time to open hearts than it does a checkbook, so let's get started.

Will you be one of Santa's Secret Helpers? Could you please help me remind the adults that Christmas is about love?

The love of caring.

The love of sharing.

The love of each other.

We need the wonderful loving feelings that start at Christmastime to last all year. We need the true meaning of Christmas to return and make the whole world better.

Every time you see me, I hope you remember what SANTA stands for and

what Christmas is really about. Please, tell everyone. I know we can do this!

Thanks for your help.

Merry Christmas!

Love, Santa

P.S.   You can share my secret with everybody.

Savior's Atonement–Necessity To All"

Captain Clyde turned to Santa. "This letter is good," he said.

"Great!" Mark shouted.

"Any suggestions?" Captain Clyde asked the elves.

"Yes. Let's get it to the kids right away!" Beverly yelled.

"Yeah!" everyone responded.

"It's a go! Three cheers," Captain Clyde said.

"Hip, hip, hurray! Hip, hip, hurray! Hip, hip, hurray!" Everyone shouted.

"Cookies for all. It's time to celebrate!" Santa said.

They laughed. They ate. They sang and danced. After the celebration, the elves got back to work making wonderful surprises full of love.

~ ~ ~

"Pssssst, Anna," Larry whispered. "I wonder what Claus stands for?"

We can do it!

For God so loved the world,
that He gave His only begotten Son,
that whosoever believes in Him should not perish,
but have everlasting life. John 3:16

Jesus said: Love one another; as I have loved you. John 13:34